Original title:
In the Interest of Letting Go

Copyright © 2024 Book Fairy Publishing
All rights reserved.

Editor: Theodor Taimla
Author: Sandra Squirrel
ISBN HARDBACK: 978-9916-759-60-8
ISBN PAPERBACK: 978-9916-759-61-5

The Last Embrace

Beneath the twilight's tender glow,
Two hearts met in a fleeting show,
A whisper soft, a final trace,
Held tightly in the last embrace.

Stars above began to weep,
As silence through the night did creep,
A sorrow deep, a love misplaced,
In shadows of that last embrace.

Eyes that shimmered, tears concealed,
A chapter closed, a fate revealed,
Memories danced in solemn grace,
Wrapped gently in the last embrace.

Echoes of Yesterday

In corridors where shadows play,
Whispers glide, and voices sway,
Each step we take, the echoes stay,
Resounding from our yesterday.

A melody of days long past,
In heart and mind these moments last,
Through fields of dreams, we softly stray,
Chasing echoes of yesterday.

The crescent moon, a silent guide,
Through nights where lost hopes often hide,
Yet in the dawn, as skies turn gray,
We find the echoes of yesterday.

Unclasped Hands

Beneath the willow's weeping strands,
Two souls once joined now unclasped hands,
A tender touch in shifting sands,
Farewell whispered, love disbands.

Leaves flutter in a silent plea,
As broken hearts set each other free,
A bond that time could not withstand,
Shattered by these unclasped hands.

Through winding paths and distant lands,
The memories of our fleeting dance,
Linger where new love withstands,
Beyond the grasp of unclasped hands.

Fleeting Shadows

In the dusk where twilight fades,
Whispered secrets, silent trades,
Moments like forgotten blades,
Carved from fleeting shadows' shades.

A dance beneath the haunted night,
Figures blend and blur from sight,
Through the dark, a lantern's light,
Guides through fleeting shadows' plight.

As dawn breaks with golden stream,
Morning wakes the weary dream,
Yet in heart, the echoes teem,
Of the night's fleeting shadows' gleam.

The Unwritten Goodbye

In silent rooms where whispers fade,
We left our words on scattered page,
A chapter closed, both hearts refrained,
In quiet moments, we disengage.

Our gazes met, an unsaid plea,
A farewell etched in memory,
No voice to break what once was free,
An echo lost in reverie.

A journey shared in twilight's glow,
Now shadows fall where dreams would go,
Unfinished lines we couldn't show,
In silence, hearts began to slow.

Flowing with the Tide

Oceans whisper secrets old,
Sunrise tales in dawn's soft gold,
Currents carry hopes untold,
Life, a story to unfold.

Sailing through the waves of time,
Horizons bright, dreams climb,
Tides may turn in nature's rhyme,
Each new swell a hopeful chime.

From shore to shore, our paths may stride,
With open hearts and eyes wide,
In this vast sea, our souls confide,
Together, flowing with the tide.

Unraveled Threads

Threads of fate in colors bright,
Woven tales in dark and light,
Time's keen scissors swift to bite,
Unweave the fabric of the night.

Patterns lost to winds that blow,
Strands of dreams in restless flow,
Hands can't mend what hearts don't know,
Unraveled lives in shadows grow.

Yet in the fray, new forms arise,
Broken threads bring fresh surprise,
From chaos spun, new dreams comprise,
A tapestry beneath our skies.

Beyond the Horizon

Past the line where oceans kiss,
Horizons blend in twilight's bliss,
Dreamers' hearts all seek in this,
A world beyond the precipice.

Mountains touch the azure skies,
Where eagles soar and spirits rise,
Beyond the clouds, adventure lies,
A realm unseen by waking eyes.

Step beyond the known and plain,
Feel the pulse of life's refrain,
In distant lands, joy and pain,
Beyond the horizon, we remain.

Shadowless Paths

In moonlit silver's grace,
Where shadows dare not tread,
There lies a calm embrace,
Where silent hopes are fed.

A journey through the veil,
No footprints leave a mark,
Beyond the world's travail,
In realms forever dark.

The stars above do guide,
Their whispers soft and clear,
Through paths that seem so wide,
Far from the world of fear.

Each step a breath of light,
In shadowless domain,
Where morning greets the night,
Amidst the gentle rain.

Beyond the Horizon

Beyond the rolling sea,
Where sky and water blend,
Lies worlds of mystery,
Where every tale can mend.

The sun dips into gold,
A promise of the day,
Adventure there untold,
In lands so far away.

Mountains kiss the sky,
Their peaks a dreamer's call,
Horizons whispering by,
Where dreams refuse to fall.

The winds of fate do blow,
A breeze both warm and cold,
To where our hopes must go,
In stories yet untold.

Resonance of Release

A heart that's turned to song,
Its burdens cast away,
In melodies so strong,
Where sorrow finds its sway.

The echoes of the past,
Resound in tones of grace,
In moments that will last,
Beyond this fleeting space.

Notes of freedom rise,
In symphony of dreams,
Where truth and beauty lies,
And all is as it seems.

The chords of life entwine,
In harmony's embrace,
Where every pain's a sign,
Of music's gentle place.

Breath of Liberation

A whisper on the breeze,
Of freedom's gentle touch,
That brings the soul to ease,
And lifts the spirit much.

With every breath we take,
A step into the light,
Where chains of fate do break,
And shadows take to flight.

The dawn of each new day,
A promise of release,
Where worries melt away,
And heartache finds its peace.

As freedom we inhale,
Its essence pure and bright,
We write our own new tale,
In morning's softest light.

Glimpse of Tomorrow

The dawn whispers softly, in hues untold,
A canvas unpainted, beginnings unfold.
Dreams interwoven, in morning's first light,
Hope rises anew, in the arms of the night.

Paths yet uncharted, horizons so wide,
Mid dreams of the future, reality hides.
Through mist and shadows, the spirit does weave,
Glimping tomorrow, what hearts might achieve.

Moments now fleeting, as time races by,
Stars in the distance, bright in the sky.
With every step forward, a story unplanned,
Footfalls of progress, mark a new land.

Clouds Adrift

Whispers of wind through the valleys so deep,
Embracing the clouds as they softly sweep.
Over the mountains, through azure skies,
Nature's ballet, in a transient disguise.

Ephemeral patterns, a dance without end,
Symbols of dreams, on breezes they wend.
Reflecting the sunlight in quivering gleam,
A serenade whispered, an aerial dream.

Mirages fleeting, they journey afar,
Lost in the heavens, where distance is star.
Comforting shadows, ever so slight,
A moment suspended in ethereal light.

No Longer Bound

From chains unshackled, we rise, we soar,
Beyond all the confines of fears once bore.
A spirit set free from the shadows' grip,
Embracing the world with each liberated step.

Cages lie empty, the doors swung wide,
No longer in darkness do we choose to hide.
Wings spread open, in the winds' embrace,
No barriers hold us, euphoria's chase.

Breaking the silence, a triumphant cry,
Echoing freely against the sky.
Boundless the horizon, the future unframed,
Seeking new frontiers where dreams are named.

Fragments of Flight

Splinters of starlight, scattered on high,
Glimpses of freedom in the moonlit sky.
Each tiny fragment, a piece of a dream,
Lost to the night in a silvery stream.

Birds in twilight, their shadows take wing,
Songs of existence in the twilight sing.
Trails of whispered wishes in the breeze,
Fragments of flight between the trees.

Hearts take to the wind, a dance of delight,
Once tethered to earth, now out of sight.
In every heartbeat, a rhythm so light,
Traces of sorrow dissolve in the night.

Unmoored Desires

In twilight's hush, where dreams conspire,
Lies a sea of unmoored desires.
Waves of longing, endless, wide,
Whisper secrets the stars can't hide.

Hearts set sail on fervent tides,
Seeking shores where love abides.
Tempests roar, yet still they yearn,
For a beacon's tender burn.

Whispers mingle with the breeze,
Binding fates to distant seas.
In the depths of midnight blue,
Thoughts of you, forever true.

Unclasped Hands

In the silence of the dusk,
Where shadows play and memories rust,
Unclasped hands, lost in time,
Wander paths of love's decline.

Echoes of a touch, once near,
Fade away like twilight's tear.
Silent promises, now stray,
In the dark, they drift away.

Through the veil of night, we stare,
Seeking solace, empty air.
Yet, in dreams, we still enclose,
Unclasped hands that time bestows.

Unveiling Horizons

When dawn unfolds its golden light,
And shadows flee the realm of night,
New horizons rise, unveiled,
Secrets of the earth exhaled.

Every peak and valley low,
Tells a tale of ebb and flow.
Journeys start with steps unknown,
Paths to places yet unshown.

As horizons stretch and bend,
To the distant world's end,
Hope's horizon, ever clear,
Whispers 'Forward, have no fear.'

The Fadeaway

In the quiet, soft decay,
Where shadows start their slow ballet,
Echoes of the day recede,
Into night they gently bleed.

Memories in twilight's glow,
Shimmer faint, then ebb and flow.
Time, a whisper, slips through hands,
Unseen footprints in the sands.

As the stars take up their post,
Guardians of what we boast,
In the fadeaway, we find,
Peace in what we've left behind.

Sighs of Solitude

In the stillness of the night,
Shadows merge with fading light,
Whispers float on silent air,
Loneliness, a dark affair.

Stars above in distant gleam,
Echo dreams we dare to dream,
In the heart, a quiet song,
Yearns for where we once belong.

Moonlit paths that lead astray,
Guide the soul to find its way,
Through the realms of silent tears,
Memories of bygone years.

A Soft Detachment.

Gently falls the evening dew,
As the sky turns deep and blue,
Breezes hum a lullaby,
Softly, we say goodbye.

Petals drift from roses bright,
Kissed by fading rays of light,
Even love can softly fade,
In the shadows it is laid.

Sea waves whisper on the shore,
Tales of love forevermore,
Yet the heart knows gentle sighs,
In each moment that it flies.

Whispering Goodbyes

Softly spoken, gentle words,
Carry on like wandering birds,
Through the wind they drift and rise,
Whispering their sweet goodbyes.

Leaves that fall from autumn trees,
Dance with grace upon the breeze,
Echoes of the times gone by,
Whispering their last goodbye.

Moments flashed in golden rays,
Scatter in the twilight haze,
Sweet as dreams of summer skies,
Whispering those last goodbyes.

Fading Footsteps

Footsteps tread on paths unknown,
Through the silent forest grown,
Echoes linger in the air,
Of the times when we were there.

Branches sway and leaves do part,
In the shadows lies the heart,
Memories in whispers greet,
Fading footsteps, bittersweet.

Wander through the misty dawn,
Seek the places we have gone,
In the quiet paths we tread,
Footsteps fading, softly led.

Vanishing Traces

Footprints in the sand, a fleeting mark,
Washed away by tides, embracing dark.
Echoes of laughter, whispers in time,
Moments once vivid, now slowly unwind.

Clouds drift across a sky once so clear,
Fading memories held ever so dear.
A leaf on the wind, a fragile grace,
Each step we take leaves vanishing trace.

Sunsets blaze with fiery gold hues,
Colors blend in a seamless fuse.
Night descends, stars softly call,
Shadows stretch tall as twilight falls.

Dreams that dance and soon slip away,
Silent ghosts of an old yesterday.
Crescent moons and autumn's cold embrace,
Life's imprints fade, leaving no trace.

Unburdened Voyage

Cast off the weight of burdens past,
Set sail into horizons vast.
With wind's sweet song and ocean's roar,
Embark on journeys never tried before.

Stars above guide through the night,
A beacon for the heart's true light.
Set your course where dreams reside,
On tranquil seas, where spirits glide.

Leave behind the chains that bind,
Embrace the call of the open mind.
Mountains tall and valleys deep,
Secret wonders for you to keep.

Adventure in the breeze's touch,
The freedom that you crave so much.
Let your soul take wing and fly,
Unburdened voyage through endless sky.

Weightless Dreams

In realms where light and shadow blend,
Weightless dreams have no end.
Floating on a whisper's tune,
Among the stars and silver moon.

Close your eyes and drift to sleep,
Where secrets of the night do keep.
Hopes and wishes gently gleam,
In the softness of a weightless dream.

Mystic paths through twilight's veil,
Winds of magic fill your sail.
Boundless skies and endless streams,
Loss and longing fade in dreams.

Hearts are free, the mind at peace,
In dreams where worries find release.
Through these realms, on wings you soar,
Weightless dreams held evermore.

Liberation Song

Rise up with the morning sun,
A new day's battle just begun.
Voices strong and spirits high,
Sing the song, let freedom fly.

Chains are broken with a cry,
Wings unfurl to claim the sky.
Each heartbeat drums its own refrain,
Release the soul from endless pain.

Marching forward, side by side,
With hope that music can't divide.
Through the strife, the road is long,
But we endure with liberation's song.

Celebrate the fight we've won,
The dawn of a new era begun.
In unity, our voices ring,
Liberation song we proudly sing.

Releasing Echoes

In the quiet of the night,
Where dreams and hopes reside,
Soft whispers take their flight,
On winds that never chide.

Through valleys deep and wide,
And mountains tall and grand,
Echoes softly glide,
Across this timeless land.

A melody of yesteryears,
With tales both old and new,
Resonates with silent tears,
In colors pale and blue.

Voices from the shadows,
Unseen yet always near,
Release their silent audio,
To hearts both far and clear.

In every breath that heaves,
In every heart that yearns,
Echoes from the leaves,
As life around us turns.

Shadows Vanished

Once shadows cloaked the dawn,
In veils so dark and deep,
Yet now those shades are gone,
In light, no longer weep.

The morning sun ascends,
To banish ghostly dreams,
Its golden light extends,
To weave enchanting gleams.

Where darkness held its sway,
Now warmth and clarity,
Guide us through the day,
With serene charity.

Glimmers paint the skies,
With hues of amber bright,
As shadows bid goodbyes,
Lost in the morning light.

In every heart that sighs,
In every soul that's free,
Find the light that flies,
To chase what shadows flee.

Breaking Free of Chains

In the depths of silent night,
Where chains once held so tight,
A spark ignites a light,
Guiding to new heights.

Bound by fears and doubts,
By unseen, heavy weights,
In rising cries and shouts,
A heart emancipates.

Each link begins to shatter,
Beneath the strength inside,
As courage starts to matter,
And hope no longer hides.

Through battles hard and fierce,
In steps of sheer resolve,
Chains dissolve to pierce,
Into a life evolved.

No longer held or tied,
By fears that once restrained,
In freedom we abide,
Breaking free of chains.

Spirit Unbound

A spirit in the breeze,
Unbound by earthly tether,
It dances with the trees,
In graceful, airy feather.

The skies receive its song,
A hymn of boundless flight,
From dusk till break of dawn,
It soars in pure delight.

Unchained by time or rules,
It ventures far and wide,
Beyond the cunning fools,
With dreams its only guide.

In freedom's endless trance,
Its journey is profound,
In every glint and glance,
A spirit truly unbound.

With hearts aloft and clear,
Embrace the path ahead,
As spirits rise and cheer,
To skies they boldly tread.

Liberating Echoes

In the quiet, whispers break,
Freeing minds from anchored dreams.
Ripples on a still heart's lake,
Banished are the silent screams.

Voices rise, an echo's flight,
Boundless as the morning sun,
Shadows flee the dawn's first light,
Chains of darkness come undone.

Thoughts untethered, take their leave,
Roaming through the open skies.
Lost no more in webs we weave,
Burdens lift with liberated sighs.

Harmony in scattered tones,
Unity from voices lone.
In our hearts, a chorus lives,
Binding all that freedom gives.

Gentle Liberation

A tender touch, a whisper soft,
Breaks the chains that bind the heart,
Wings of grace, they lift aloft,
Pain and sorrow now depart.

Love's sweet breath, a gentle breeze,
Guides us to a brighter shore,
From our doubts it brings release,
Peace and solace, evermore.

In the quiet of the night,
Silent dreams begin to rise,
Casting off the chains of plight,
Soaring in the starry skies.

Hope anew, each dawn displays,
Frees the soul to dance and sing,
Washing tears of yesterday,
Gentle hands of love will bring.

Shattered Wings

Once I flew on winds so high,
Dreams were woven, reaching far,
But a storm darkened the sky,
Shattered wings, a falling star.

Grounded now, on earth I tread,
Fragments pierce my weary soul,
Where the light and dark have bled,
Striving still to make me whole.

Through the struggle, there is grace,
Every piece a story tells,
Wounds that heal, a tender trace,
From these falls, a strength compels.

One day soon I'll rise again,
With new wings to touch the skies,
Shattered once, but not the end,
From the ashes, I'll arise.

Wandering Souls

In the night, our spirits roam,
Seeking what we can't define,
Far from hearth and far from home,
Guided by the stars' faint shine.

Every path a shadowed line,
Every choice, a whispered call,
Seekers in a grand design,
Finding meaning in it all.

Wandering souls in endless quest,
Hungering for truth and light,
Never still, we're driven, pressed,
Through the day and through the night.

In our searching, we are found,
Lost in worlds yet ours to claim,
Footsteps on this sacred ground,
Wandering souls, untamed, unnamed.

Clouds of Freedom

In skies so wide they roam,
With whispers soft as dream,
They write the endless poem,
Of rivers, fields, and beam.

They drift with no restraint,
Above the grounded care,
Each one a transient saint,
In azure vastness, fair.

Spirits of air and grace,
Their forms a fleeting dance,
Unbound by time or place,
They seize each given chance.

Eternal wanderers they,
In ballet light as air,
From dawn to end of day,
They weave through thought and prayer.

No chains, no ties, no plight,
Their journey never ends,
In freedom pure and bright,
To all the world extends.

Breaking Night

The stars begin to fade,
As dawn ignites the sky,
In shadows still they wade,
But morning's near reply.

Darkness yields to light,
A canvas freshly spun,
Through whispers of the night,
Emerges the new sun.

Soft hues in pastel dreams,
Spill o'er the quiet land,
Where twilight's final beams,
Release their tender hand.

A symphony unfolds,
In tones both bright and fair,
The silent night remolds,
To morning's gentle air.

Awakens life anew,
In golden, early rays,
The world, in glist'ning dew,
Greets the coming phase.

Echoes on the Wind

Whispers in the breeze,
Of times long gone by,
Among the silent trees,
Their secrets softly sigh.

Carried through the vale,
By winds of yesteryear,
Their stories never stale,
In memories they steer.

The voices of the past,
In gentle breaths they spin,
Within the branches cast,
As echoes on the wind.

Through valleys, over hills,
They travel far and wide,
A song that never stills,
A guide by nature's side.

In every gust they weave,
A tale that never dies,
Forever they conceive,
New ways for hearts to rise.

Silent Sky

Above, a quiet dome,
No sound disrupts the night,
It feels eternal, home,
In deep and tranquil light.

Stars like whispers shine,
Their glow a silent call,
A vast and old design,
Unites them one and all.

No noise to stir the air,
Just peace in every fold,
A stillness soft and rare,
Beneath the night's pure gold.

Each star a muted voice,
In cosmic harmony,
Through silence they rejoice,
In endless symphony.

Beneath this muted realm,
Our thoughts become so clear,
No chaos overwhelms,
Just calmness, ever near.

Unchained Melody

In twilight's gentle, quiet sway,
A song of love begins to play,
Soft whispers on the evening breeze,
Unchained, our spirits find their ease.

Your voice, a melody so pure,
In fleeting moments, we endure,
Bound by notes that gently rise,
Echoes lingering in the skies.

From heart to heart, the tune ascends,
A harmony that never ends,
Each chord a promise, soft and true,
Of endless love, just me and you.

The night draws close, yet still we sing,
Two souls in perfect symphony,
Unchained by time, unbound by fear,
Together, love, forever near.

So let the music take its flight,
Beyond the realms of day and night,
In every note, our hearts entwine,
Eternal, endless, ever mine.

The Last Wave

Upon the shore, where dreams reside,
The waves embrace the evening tide,
With every crest, a story told,
Of loves once young, now gently old.

The sea, a mirror of the skies,
Reflects the tears in wanderers' eyes,
A symphony of wind and foam,
A bittersweet, eternal home.

With every wave that softly breaks,
A memory stirs, a heartache wakes,
The ocean's song, both wild and free,
Carries whispers of what used to be.

Beneath the stars, the world is still,
Yet waves persist, with boundless will,
Echoes of laughter, sighs of pain,
Eternal cycles wax and wane.

As dawn approaches, light and frail,
The last wave tells a final tale,
Of love and loss, of dreams that crave,
Within the heart of the last wave.

Shifting Sands

Upon the dunes, where time does play,
The shifting sands do softly sway,
Each grain a story, old and new,
In patterns kissed by morning dew.

Beneath the sun's relentless glare,
The sands move on, without a care,
Forming landscapes, ever changed,
In nature's works, so rearranged.

Footprints fade with every breeze,
Forgotten trails among the seas,
Yet memories stay within the hearts,
Of wanderers who leave their marks.

The desert blossoms with the night,
Its secrets hidden from our sight,
In shifting sands, the past remains,
Eternal whispers in the grains.

So wander on, through time and space,
In shifting sands, life leaves its trace,
A journey where our souls expand,
In the embrace of shifting sand.

The Freedom of Flight

Above the hills, beyond the stream,
A realm where only eagles dream,
The azure sky, so vast and bright,
Unveils the freedom of the flight.

With wings outstretched, they soar so high,
A dance of grace against the sky,
Through clouds they weave, in currents ride,
In nature's arms they gently glide.

The world below, a distant blur,
As breezes ruffle feathered fur,
Each rise and fall, a story spun,
Of adventures, yet begun.

From peak to peak, they navigate,
Escaping chains of earthly fate,
To where horizons kiss the sea,
A boundless world, forever free.

So much to learn from skies above,
A life unbound, defined by love,
In every flight, the truth revealed,
The freedom found, the spirit healed.

A New Dawn Beckons

With night's embrace now fading,
The horizon's glow ignites,
A new dawn beckons warmly,
Unveiling day from night.

Soft whispers of the morning,
Stir leaves with gentle grace,
Awakening the slumber,
Of earth's serene embrace.

Birds soar with aspirations,
Across the sky so wide,
A tapestry of colors,
Embracing life's great tide.

Each ray a hopeful promise,
A chance to start anew,
Underneath the vast expanse,
Where dreams and hopes accrue.

Embrace the dawn that's calling,
With every breath you take,
For in this gentle morning,
New paths we'll surely make.

Vanish in the Night

In shadows deep and silent,
Where moonlight casts its spell,
Whispers of the night time,
In secrets softly tell.

Stars like shards of diamonds,
Pierce the midnight sky,
Silent serenading,
As the world goes by.

Winds dance in the darkness,
Through trees with ancient might,
Carrying the echoes,
That vanish in the night.

Dreams float like fragile feathers,
Upon the velvet breeze,
Embraced by cosmic rhythms,
That put the mind at ease.

In the realm of whispers,
Where shadows softly fall,
We vanish in the night time,
As dreams and stars enthrall.

Breaking Dawn

Night's tapestry is lifting,
A glow begins to rise,
Breaking dawn approaches,
With hues that mesmerize.

The silence gently ruptures,
With morning's tender sigh,
A symphony of waking,
Beneath the boundless sky.

Dreams dissipate like morning mist,
As sunlight starts to creep,
Awakening each whisper,
From the land of sleep.

Colors blend and merge again,
Painting skies anew,
As dawn breaks with a promise,
And life begins to brew.

Embrace the birth of morning,
With every graceful light,
For in the glow of breaking,
Lies endless new delight.

Casting Away

Waves whisper secrets softly,
To shores they've kissed for years,
Casting away the worries,
And all the hidden fears.

A boat that gently sways there,
Upon the ocean's crest,
Carries dreams and promises,
In slumbered waves' caress.

The sailor's heart beats steady,
With every ebb and flow,
Casting away the burdens,
To where the winds will blow.

Stars guide the quiet journey,
Across the tranquil sea,
A voyage toward the horizon,
Where heart and spirit flee.

On waters' vast expanse now,
Through night's and day's embrace,
Casting away their anchors,
To find a better place.

Quiet Revolution

In whispers of the morning breeze,
The seeds of change begin to grow,
Not thunderous, but silent pleas,
Transforming silently below.

New ideas in stillness rise,
Echoes soft, but hearts they stir,
A subtle shift, a gentle prize,
Where dreams and actions start to blur.

Silent voices, calm and brave,
Gather strength in unity's form,
Breaking free from doubt's dark cave,
Ushering in a hopeful norm.

Through the quiet, power's found,
In each step of silent quest,
Bound by peace, our movements sound,
To build a world that's truly blessed.

So let the silent revolution turn,
With every whispered, heartfelt plea,
For in the gentle change we yearn,
Lies the path to true liberty.

The Final Breath

In twilight's calm, where shadows creep,
A breath, once strong, begins to fade,
The soul prepares its gentle leap,
From earth's weight, to heavens made.

A final sigh, a whispered name,
Through starlit skies, a soul ascends,
Releasing all from earthly claim,
Where boundless peace and light transcends.

Memories drift like autumn leaves,
In hearts of those who linger here,
The pain subsides, though love still grieves,
Yet in peace, there's naught to fear.

With every breath, life's tale concludes,
A gentle pause before the new,
In realms unknown, the heart renews,
Where past and present blend to view.

Farewell the world of fleeting strife,
Embrace the calm that follows death,
For in the end, what gifts us life,
Becomes one cherished, final breath.

Bearing the Unseen

Invisible burdens, unseen chains,
We carry them in silence deep,
Through life's uncharted, stormy plains,
And secrets that our souls must keep.

Behind each smile, a hidden scar,
Wounds that time and love will bind,
Yet in our hearts, we wander far,
Seeking solace we cannot find.

In whispered prayers upon the night,
We cast our fears into the wind,
Hoping dreams will set things right,
And mend the places where we've sinned.

Strength is found in unseen wars,
Battled quietly within,
For every heart its story stores,
Of bearing places we've been.

So hold the hand of those you meet,
For unseen weights they too may bear,
Together, make their burdens beat,
And lighten sorrows they must wear.

Sunset Dissolve

As day dissolves into the night,
The sky ignites in hues of red,
A painter's dream in fading light,
Where sun and shadows, silent led.

The world slows down in twilight's hue,
Where whispers of the evening's song,
Carry peace in shades of blue,
To places hearts have searched for long.

Golden rays in final dance,
Bid farewell to the waking day,
In this tranquil, twilight trance,
Night's calm begins its gentle play.

Stars emerge, a cosmic glow,
Guiding dreams and restless minds,
In sunset's peace, our spirits grow,
Leaving worldly cares behind.

So let the night embrace the past,
As sunset's colors softly blend,
For every dusk, a peace so vast,
Where day and night in harmony end.

Shifting Sands

Across the dune where shadows sweep,
The desert whispers secrets deep.
In grains of gold, its tales they weave,
Of times long past, of souls who grieve.

The wind, a sculptor, shapes the land,
With tender touch, and gentle hand.
It carves our dreams, our fleeting plans,
In timeless dance, of shifting sands.

Mirages play, in heat's embrace,
Where thirsty hearts find solace, grace.
Oases bloom, with life unplanned,
Then fade away, in shifting sands.

Stars peer down, with ancient gaze,
Their light a guide, through night's dark maze.
We wander on, in vast expanse,
Our lives but blinks, in shifting sands.

Sunset Surrenders

The sky ignites with hues of red,
Where day and night in silence wed.
A fleeting glow, day's final guise,
Before the dark, bids light goodbye.

Beneath this dome of amber hues,
The world transcends its earthly blues.
In twilight's grip, all worries cease,
As sunset surrenders to the peace.

Mountains bathed in crimson light,
Their shadowed forms now soft, contrite.
In evening's hush, the earth respires,
As sunset surrenders to night's choir.

The ocean mirrors skies alight,
Its waves, a dance of day and night.
In twilight's kiss, the stars conspire,
As sunset surrenders to the night's attire.

Ephemeral Bonds

In fleeting touch, our hearts engage,
A moment's grace, within life's stage.
We find connection, pure, unplanned,
Ephemeral bonds, like grains of sand.

A glance, a smile, a whispered word,
In such brief sparks, our souls are heard.
These transient ties, so slight, so grand,
They bind our paths, ephemeral bonds.

For in life's tide, where currents flow,
We drift apart, and yet we grow.
These threads that weave our stories long,
Are fleeting notes in time's sweet song.

Though time may take these ties away,
Their echoes in our hearts will stay.
In memories, where moments stand,
We cherish our ephemeral bonds.

Fractured Chains

In shadows cast by light's embrace,
We find our strength in mercy's grace.
Through trials hard and endless pains,
We break at last, our fractured chains.

A soul once bound, now free to soar,
Above the scars that came before.
With every step, new courage gains,
Emancipated from fractured chains.

The past a ghost, in distant lands,
With open heart, we make our stand.
In healing's touch, new life remains,
We rewrite fate, from fractured chains.

Through darkness deep, a guiding star,
Leads us to who we truly are.
In unity, we mend our frames,
Together breaking fractured chains.

Faded Portraits

In a book of memories, dusty and old,
Whispers of stories, long since told,
Faces smile from yellowed seams,
Echoes of laughter, woven in dreams.

Time takes its toll, as colors flee,
Sepia shadows where life used to be,
Stillness captured in a captured glance,
Haunted by what's left to chance.

Eyes once bright, now hazed in gray,
Moments stolen, night and day,
Canvas of time, worn and frayed,
Love's last whisper, slow to fade.

Hope and sorrow, mingled in hues,
Left behind, like forgotten muse,
Silent witnesses to stories past,
In frames eternal, they forever last.

Silent rooms where they reside,
Gone are days when life did stride,
Yet in those faded, fragile scenes,
Lives the essence of aged dreams.

Final Pages

Ink has dried on a tale complete,
Lines of love, and life's heartbeat,
Each chapter turned, a world unfurled,
Now closed, a silent curled pearl.

Whispers rest on the parchment old,
Stories of hearts both shy and bold,
Adventures end with life's last stage,
Bound forever on these final page.

Dreams once wild, now gently close,
Hushed as twilight's fading rose,
At journey's end, where shadows lie,
Stars will light the evening sky.

Farewells spoken in twilight's glow,
Farewells we know but cannot show,
Voices softly in memories rage,
Silent echoes in their cage.

Yet life remains in memory's hold,
In stories told, forever bold,
Final pages, tales complete,
Until the next two souls greet.

Ephemeral Touch

As dawn breaks with tender light,
Moments fleeting, pure and bright,
A touch of life, soft as breeze,
Gone too quick, like autumn leaves.

Fingers trace the edge of dreams,
Glimmers in the morning beams,
Transient whispers, barely known,
Ephemeral touch, swiftly flown.

Time's embrace in passing glance,
Lost in rhythm, life's danse,
Beauty found within a touch,
Yet it fades, though we clutch.

Delicate as a snowflake's kiss,
Brief, like a moment's bliss,
Transient, like a shadow's stride,
Yet eternal in the heart's tide.

Teach us well, their fleeting ways,
Life in tiny, intricate displays,
Every touch, a world inside,
Ephemeral, yet our hearts confide.

Unlocked Souls

Behind the doors, hearts kept tight,
Dreams and fears, locked from sight,
A whisper calls to break the mold,
To open hearts, to dare be bold.

In twilight's glow, shadows dance,
Souls unlocked, given a chance,
Barriers fall as truth takes flight,
In newfound freedom, pure delight.

Eyes that meet, secrets shared,
In the stillness, hearts have bared,
Unlock the chambers where they hide,
Merge in love, stride by stride.

Keys of hope, and trust, and grace,
Open locks in life's tight space,
Journey's start, where barriers break,
In shared dreams, new paths we make.

Let them flow, let barriers cease,
In unlocked souls, find true peace,
Love's grand dance in open skies,
Souls unbound, in tender sighs.

Wings of Release

In twilight's gentle, soft embrace,
I find a path, my heart's own place.
With every step, the shadows cease,
As dreams take flight on wings of release.

Beneath the stars, where whispers play,
Each burden's weight, a memory fades away.
In boundless skies, our spirits tease,
Unshackled by the breeze, wings of release.

From ancient oaks, the leaves depart,
A symbol of the untamed heart.
In every fall, there's sweet increase,
A dance of fate on wings of release.

Moonlight's kiss on tranquil streams,
Reflects our hopes, forever gleams.
In silent nights, our souls find peace,
Bound in the flight of wings of release.

Above the clouds, in realms so free,
We find our truth, our destiny.
Together, love our final lease,
Eternal bond on wings of release.

Fading into Dawn

The night is long, a still repose,
In shadows deep, where dreams disclose.
A whispered wish, a secret drawn,
We set our sights on fading into dawn.

Through mist and dark, our spirits wade,
In fleeting moments, fears allayed.
With every breath, a new life spawned,
We greet the light, fading into dawn.

Stars retreat with tender sighs,
As morning's hues caress the skies.
In silent awe, the world is spawned,
And we, with it, are fading into dawn.

From midnight's shroud, our hearts emerge,
In harmony, our spirits surge.
Together strong, forever gone,
Our new horizon, fading into dawn.

In amber light, we find our way,
The promise of a brighter day.
With every step, the night forgone,
We meet our dreams, fading into dawn.

Unveiled Horizons

Beyond the veil of mists and haze,
Lies endless skies, our hearts will graze.
With courage found, our fears are gone,
We journey forth to unveiled horizons.

Each step we take, a path unknown,
In unity, we're not alone.
With every dawn, the night withdrawn,
We walk as one to unveiled horizons.

Through valleys deep and mountains high,
The endless world beneath the sky.
Our spirits guide, we'll carry on,
Forever drawn to unveiled horizons.

In every star, a tale untold,
In every breeze, our fates unfold.
With hope as bright as morning's yawn,
We chase the dream of unveiled horizons.

Together bound, hearts intertwined,
In love and life, the journey bind.
With passion fierce and thoughts upon,
We set our gaze to unveiled horizons.

The Frayed Cord

In silent rooms where whispers dwell,
A story of the heart we tell.
A love once strong, now gently stored,
Bound by time, the frayed cord.

With every tear, a memory leaks,
In quiet nights, the soul it seeks.
A tethered bond, no longer soared,
Now drifts along, the frayed cord.

From tender touch to distant glance,
A echoed dance of lost romance.
In moments gone, the heart explored,
The delicate thread, the frayed cord.

Through years of joy and hinted pain,
In sunlight's loss, and autumn's gain.
Our stories etched, in hearts adored,
Yet still it holds, the frayed cord.

And though it frays, it never breaks,
In time's embrace, a love remakes.
Renewed in strength, the past restored,
We heal and mend, the frayed cord.

Effortless Drift

Beneath the twilight's gentle thrall,
The river whispers stories old,
Of dreams that wander, softly fall,
In waters cool, through shades of gold.

The breeze a tender hand extends,
To guide the leaves in lazy dance,
Where time, it bends and gently mends,
Of silent whispers, in a trance.

Forgotten shores in twilight's veil,
Where echoes fade, and shadows blend,
On destiny's uncharted trail,
Each ripple finds its woven end.

Stars awaken in night's embrace,
Their light a quilt on waters spun,
Imbue the drifts with silent grace,
As dark and light meld into one.

Through sleepless nights and days anew,
The current's course remains unswayed,
Effortless drift, a path is true,
In nature's arms forever laid.

Passing Clouds

In fields of endless fleeting light,
They waltz across the azure seas,
With whispered tales of day and night,
In tender touch with soaring breeze.

They change, they float, they fade away,
Ephemeral like dreams of glass,
Heed not the clock, nor night, nor day,
Through cosmic dances, they do pass.

Upon the mountains grand and high,
The passing clouds their shadows cast,
A stream of thoughts against the sky,
Moments fleeting, yet will last.

With every turn, a story ends,
Reborn in shapes anew they form,
Among the winds and gentle bends,
Their transient dance, a timeless norm.

So let us watch and learn their ways,
The art of being here and now,
From passing clouds in sunlit rays,
To peace, our hearts shall gently bow.

A Gentle Dispatch

A letter sealed in morning's light,
With words of love on paper penned,
It travels far through day and night,
To reach a heart, a hand, a friend.

The ink a river of the soul,
Each line a bridge across the void,
In tender whispers to console,
A gentle dispatch to be enjoyed.

Through rain and sun and winding path,
The journey's long, the miles refrain,
Yet every word withstands the wrath,
Of time and space, of joy and pain.

When hands receive this token dear,
A smile blooms upon the face,
For messages of hope appear,
In written lines, a warm embrace.

So send we forth with tender care,
Our heartfelt thoughts, our silent song,
A gentle dispatch through the air,
To those apart, where hearts belong.

Severed Strings

The moonlight played on silver strings,
A melody of lost goodbyes,
An echo through the night it sings,
Of stories told in silent cries.

With every note the bond did break,
A severed string, a heart undone,
In shadows deep we lay awake,
And mourn the fading of the sun.

Once woven tight in love's embrace,
The tapestry now pulled apart,
A song of sorrow, lined with grace,
A severed bond, a fractured heart.

Yet through the night, the music stays,
A whispering of what once was,
A haunting tune of bygone days,
In silent tears, we trace the cause.

And when the dawn begins to climb,
A new refrain the morning brings,
From ashes there, in grief and time,
We'll find repair for severed strings.

Unwoven Threads

In whispers weave unseen, the strands they part,
A tapestry undone, yet still a work of art,
Fate's loom unknots the tales we once held tight,
In twilight's hush, the threads dissolve in night.

Memories lie in fragments, scattered wide,
A quilt unraveled by the turning tide,
Yet in each fragment, echoes still reside,
Of stories told and futures yet to bide.

Each thread a dream, a hope, a silent plea,
A tapestry of what was meant to be,
Now floats upon the wind so wild and free,
Unwritten paths in life's vast tapestry.

The loom stands still, yet life goes on its way,
In warp and weft, the night turns into day,
Unwoven threads, like moments in a play,
Fade softly into dreams that drift away.

In every ending, beginnings come to light,
Unseen, yet gathering the threads of night,
Unwoven stories spark a new insight,
As dawn reshapes their hues with morning's light.

Melting Memories

Beneath the sun, where ice and heart both thaw,
Memories melt, revealing what we saw,
Visions fade, like frost in morning's breath,
Yet in their wake, new dreams defy their death.

Time's warm embrace dissolves the frozen past,
Each drop a whisper of what couldn't last,
But in the pool of shattered moments cast,
A new reflection finds us at the last.

Each melting memory leaves behind a trace,
A silent mark within our inner space,
And as they fade, they craft a gentle lace,
Of transient beauty, delicate in grace.

The past recedes, its shadows fall away,
In quiet drips, it bids farewell to day,
But in that melting, brighter futures sway,
Awaiting dawn where hope and memory play.

Through melting memories, we find release,
As sorrows blend and transform into peace,
With every tear, a chance for new increase,
To grow and love, as fleeting moments cease.

Beneath the Burden

Beneath the burden, shoulders bow and strain,
Yet through the weight, resilience we gain,
For in the darkest hours, we find our flame,
To push beyond the limits life can name.

Every trial, a test of what we bear,
Each struggle, a testament of care,
As burdens press, they mold us in their snare,
Until we rise, unbreakable and rare.

The weight of worries, fears and silent scars,
Though heavy, shapes the strength that now is ours,
In every step, determination stars,
To forge a path through life's relentless bars.

Beneath the burden, wisdom finds its place,
In every challenge, courage sets its pace,
Our hearts, though heavy, time cannot erase,
For through the strain, we find our saving grace.

Each burden carried, yes, it leaves a mark,
But in its shadow, waits a glowing spark,
A light that guides us through the deepest dark,
And kindles hope, beneath the toughest arc.

Untethered Dreams

Untethered dreams, like stars, they drift afar,
In night's embrace, where boundless visions are,
They sail on winds of whispers, soft and clear,
Through realms of magic, far from doubt and fear.

Each dream a beacon in the vast unknown,
A seed of light in cosmos overblown,
Within their glow, new worlds are gently sown,
As dreams take flight in skies they've never known.

In sleep's embrace, the chains of day release,
Our spirits soar with an unfettered peace,
In realms where wonders never seem to cease,
Where every dream finds hope and sweet increase.

Untethered dreams, they dance with wild delight,
In bounds of night, where shadows spark with light,
They craft a tale beyond our mortal sight,
And paint our hearts with colors ever bright.

Through untethered dreams, we glimpse the vast and grand,
In their embrace, we finally understand,
That in the night, our souls find strength to stand,
As dreams enfold us with a gentle hand.

Fading Footprints

In sands of time our marks do blend,
Fleeting traces journey's end.
Waves erase, the past concealed,
Echoes lost, but dreams revealed.

Steps we take on paths unknown,
Whispers carried, seeds are sown.
History's dance, a subtle art,
Memory fades, yet warms the heart.

Within the dusk, the sun descends,
Daylight bows as night transcends.
Ephemeral paths by moonlight kissed,
Shadows speak of moments missed.

Footprints may dissolve from sight,
Leaving whispers in the night.
Legends linger, tales unfold,
Fading footprints, stories told.

Each step a chapter in the breeze,
Gone, but not lost to the seas.
Transient lives in sands discreet,
Footprints fade, hearts still beat.

Cleansing the Heart

A gentle rain, the earth caressed,
Cleansing tears, the heart expressed.
Purity flows through every scar,
Healing light where shadows are.

In streams of life, in currents clear,
Wash away each hidden tear.
Renewed spirit, fresh and bright,
Shine within the tranquil night.

The autumn leaves, like whispered dreams,
Float upon the silken streams.
Burdens lifted, light as air,
Find serenity everywhere.

A song of dawn as night departs,
Echoes deep within our hearts.
Rebirth blooms in morning's grace,
Love and peace in every place.

Let go the sorrow, let it part,
Nature's balm, it soothes the heart.
New beginnings softly start,
In the quiet, healing art.

Transcendence Over Time

In the silent halls of ages past,
Whispers of truth, they hold steadfast.
Timeless echoes, memories gleam,
Life's eternal, flowing stream.

Moments fleeting, yet they stay,
Guiding light of yesterday.
Transcendence rises, breaking bonds,
Futures woven, beyond the dawns.

Glimpses in the shadows cast,
Mirrors of the future past.
Threads of fate, they intertwine,
Destinies in rhythm rhyme.

Seasons paint the endless flight,
Stars are born from ancient night.
Cycles spin, creation's art,
Endings here, just another start.

Time's embrace, a seamless flow,
Teach us what the wise ones know.
Beyond the veils of day and night,
Transcendence lifts us, takes its flight.

Wings of Surrender

On feathered whispers, dreams alight,
Wings of surrender, take their flight.
Into skies of endless blue,
Hopes ascend, perspectives new.

Letting go of earthly weight,
Trust in winds to navigate.
Souls unbound by heavy chains,
Hearts set free above the plains.

Every breath, a liberating surge,
Boundaries dissolve and merge.
In surrender, strength we find,
Peace within, the boundless mind.

Floating high where eagles soar,
Life's vast tapestry explore.
Wings uncurled to possibilities,
In surrender, endless seas.

To the breeze we give our all,
Rising up, we never fall.
Embrace the sky, our spirit lends,
Wings of surrender, journey sends.

Unclasped Hands

In the quiet of dawn's embrace,
We part with a tender glance,
Fingers lose their gentle trace,
In the rhythm of a silent dance.

Memories linger, soft and light,
In the spaces we once knew,
Whispered secrets lose their might,
In the sky's vast azure hue.

Dreams released from grasped intent,
Float like leaves upon the breeze,
Moments shared, now softly spent,
In the hush of whispered seas.

Paths diverge, as shadows blend,
In the twilight's gentle sway,
Unclasped hands find journeys' end,
As night turns to break of day.

In the stillness, hearts do mend,
In the echoes of a song,
Love will find its way to bend,
Embracing where we once belonged.

Drifting Petals

Petals drift on winds' soft sigh,
Carrying secrets far and wide,
In their dance, a gentle lie,
Whispering stories in their glide.

Blossoms fall like fleeting dreams,
In the morn's first tender light,
Captured in the sunlight's beams,
They vanish from our sight.

Springtime's kiss, a brief delight,
Turns to whispers in the night,
Petals scattered out of sight,
Yet memories still hold them tight.

In the garden's quiet calm,
Nature sings her timeless song,
Drifting petals in her palm,
Where past and future both belong.

With each turn, a silent grace,
Petals take their path anew,
Leaving in their whispered trace,
A tender memory of you.

Silent Liberation

Chains once held us, fierce and tight,
In the shadows of our minds,
Now we step into the light,
Leaving all our fears behind.

Silent voices, now set free,
Speak of dreams and hopes reborn,
In the dawn's first blush we see,
New paths where our souls adorn.

In the stillness of this space,
We discover strength untold,
Finding in the quiet grace,
Courage that does not grow old.

Whispered breezes guide our quest,
Through the storms, and through the calm,
Every trial, a needed test,
Every wound, a healing balm.

Silent liberation's song,
Echoes in each heart that dares,
To break free and to belong,
In the love that ever bears.

The Hollow Echo

In the canyon's deep embrace,
Echoes linger, soft and low,
Whispering in the empty space,
Of the things we used to know.

Voices fade in hollow tones,
Reverberating through the air,
Shadows dance on silent stones,
Ghosts of memories everywhere.

Listen close to what they say,
In the quiet of the night,
Fragments of a yesterday,
Caught within the fading light.

Time distorts the echoed call,
Stretching moments, bending past,
In the hollow, we find all,
That was never meant to last.

Yet in every sound that stays,
Lies a secret to unearth,
Echoes guide us through the maze,
Back to where we find our worth.

Untethered Spirit

In the boundless skies, I soar,
A whisper, a wisp, an open door.
No chains to hold, no ties to bind,
Freedom's melody, pure and kind.

Winds of change beneath my wings,
Echoes of forgotten things.
I dance on dreams, where eagles dare,
In realms unseen, beyond compare.

Stars unfold in twilight's realm,
Guiding paths where I atone.
A voyager with heart aglow,
On currents high and far below.

Cloaked in night's eternal grace,
Unseen footprints leave a trace.
In whispered songs, my soul will find,
An endless journey, undefined.

Echoes fade, but spirit stays,
An eternal wanderer in cosmic maze.
With every dawn, I rise anew,
Boundless skies, and boundless view.

Fleeting Captivity

Within the cage, the heart resides,
Where shadows creep and freedom hides.
Dreams confined in silent plea,
A yearning soul, to wander free.

Bars of doubt and fears entwine,
Constrained by life's own strict design.
But in the heart, a hope can bloom,
A glimmer in the captive gloom.

Silent whispers beckon fate,
To break these chains that suffocate.
Through twilight's veil and day's disguise,
A flight awaits, past captive skies.

In night's embrace, a secret waltz,
Where spirit thrives beyond the vaults.
The cage but moment's passing phase,
A fleeting touch in life's grand maze.

And when the dawn of freedom breaks,
The heart rejoices, lighter takes.
In realms unbound, the soul now flies,
Released from fleeting captivities.

Sunset Horizons

On the edge of day, the sun reclines,
Casting hues in soft designs.
A canvas brushed with twilight's hues,
A serenade in golden views.

Mountains kiss the fading light,
Shadows lengthen, day turns night.
Whispers in the amber glow,
Tales of yonder, soft and slow.

Oceans mirror skies ablaze,
In twilight's tender, fleeting phase.
A symphony on waves' embrace,
Sunset's kiss, a lover's grace.

Birds in flight toward distant nest,
Carry dreams within their quest.
Horizon's line a gentle call,
To distant lands where night may fall.

Moments held in twilight's arms,
Softly wrapped in evening's charms.
With every sunset, hope is spun,
For dreams anew with each new sun.

Whispers of Departure

Footsteps echo down the hall,
A shadowed trace upon the wall.
Whispers soft in evening's hush,
A fleeting touch, a gentle brush.

The door now stands ajar, alone,
A silent testament of gone.
Memories linger in the air,
Between what's lost and what's still there.

Breezes carry voices past,
Of moments shared that couldn't last.
Each whisper holds a last goodbye,
Caught between the earth and sky.

Eyes that watch the fading light,
Hold the echoes of the night.
In the silence, hearts do learn,
Of tethered paths that must adjourn.

With every step, the whispers fade,
In twilight's gentle, soft cascade.
Departures weave the threads of time,
In whispered notes, both sad and fine.